Geography
of the
Near Past

BY AL YOUNG

Poetry
Dancing
The Song Turning Back Into Itself
Geography of the Near Past

Fiction
Snakes
Who Is Angelina?
Sitting Pretty

Geography of the Near Past

POEMS BY AL YOUNG

Holt, Rinehart and Winston
NEW YORK

Library of Congress Cataloging in Publication Data

Young, Al, 1939–
    Geography of the near past.

    I. Title.
PS3575.0683A17   1976   811'.5'4   75–21624
ISBN 0–03–013876–0
ISBN 0–03–013881–7 pbk.

Many of these poems, some in slightly different form, have already appeared in the following publications whose editors are thanked for permission to reprint: *Aftermath of Invisibility, California Poets Anthology* (Second Coming Press), *Counter/Measures, Decal* (Cardiff, Wales), *Dices, Egg, Epoch, Evergreen, Hambone, Iowa Review, Love (Incorporating Hate), Loveletter, Loves, Etc., Massachusetts Review, Mosaic: Literature and Ideas* (University of Manitoba Press), *New Directions 29, New Orleans Review, Obsidian, Paris Review, Place, Quarry, Sequoia, Umoja, WPA,* and *Yardbird Reader.*

FIRST EDITION

Designer: Betty Binns
PRINTED IN THE UNITED STATES OF AMERICA
10 9 8 7 6 5 4 3 2 1

*For my grandmother, Mrs. Lillian Campbell;
for Mei Nakano, Joye Crespo, & for Dave & Sheila
MacDonald whose dark green prose & pictures
brighten Waverley Street.*

Backtracking

for Arl

Ive already told you about the dance,
the wayward song, the way the moon
follows me up into bed on the chance
something might come tumbling down soon.

Well, whatll it be this time around,
what kind of silence or tight blue light
is there to be broken, gathered, or found
as winter freezes over our shoulders tonight?

The only pictures we've ever lent you,
whisper our windows being looked out of,
are of sunshine & snow you keep walking into
as you would a mirror, an eyeful of love.

What say this time I pick up your lead
& follow you back to the only real need?

Contents

The Sad Hour of Your Peace

American Glamour

Geography of the Near Past

Some Recent Fiction

Boogie with O.O. Gabugah

The
Sad Hour
of Your
Peace

Elegy

TED CUNNINGHAM (*1926-1971*)

Good morning!
Good morning!
Good morning!

This was your greeting
all day long.

Walking into your home
the first thing one noticed
was always music.

Walking into your life
the first thing one felt
was always music.

How could a man like you
not sing, not play, not dance,
not stretch mornings
into midnight?

When you gave yourself
in true matrimony
to one beautiful woman
you both made *Jet* magazine:
Black Ex-Priest Weds Ex-Nun
or words to that effect.

The real story would make
anyone's heart pound
with admiration & affirm
the sacredness of being alive.

Neither the Church
nor the Jesuit order
was expansive enough
or windowless enough
to contain the breadth
of your spirit.

You were blessed with only
one child of your own & yet
countless children must have
cherished your fatherly touch.

Good morning—
it isnt enough to simply
preach about loving the poor.

Good morning—
there's so much work to be done!

Good morning—
there's no time to waste!

"Good morning!" you sang
for the next-to-last time
to your remarkable wife
to your six-month-old daughter
to the grandmother who raised you
to all of your friends
remembered, recorded, live.

Good morning, Omaha!
Good morning, Nairobi!
Good morning, New York!
Good morning, Vatican City!
Good morning, California!
Good morning, bureaucracy!
Good morning, cancer!
Good morning, suffering!
Good morning, brothers & sisters!

Along with everything else
you taught that elegies &
memorial rituals were for
the living to console the living.
If yesterday or tomorrow
meant anything to you
you quietly never showed it.

You didnt practice selflessness,
you had it down pat & lived it
in one bright, endless morning.

This world that you moved thru
but were not attached to
is, perhaps without knowing it,
all the lonelier for your absence,
all the richer for your presence.

"Good morning!" you said.

Good morning, Ted.

For Arl
in Her Sixth Month

Cool beneath melon-colored cloth, your belly—
a joyous ripening that happens & happens,
that gently takes root & takes over,
a miracle uncelebrated under an autumn dress
that curves & falls slowly to your ankles.

As you busy yourself with backyard gardening,
humming, contained, I think of your tongue
at peace in its place; another kind of fruit,
mysterious flower behind two lips that open
for air & for exits & entrances.

                                   Perhaps if I placed
my hungry ear up next to a cantaloupe or coconut
(for hours at a time & often enough),
I'd hear a fluttering or maybe a music almost like
the story Ive heard with my ear to your belly,
a seashell history of evolution personified.

Your womb is a room where it's always afternoon.

Studio up over
In Your Ear

The radiator's hissing hot
My Smith-Corona's cleaned & oiled
with a fresh nylon ribbon
for the hard miles ahead

Gurney Norman's notes for his book
scribbled against this flaking wall
painted landlord green grow more
cryptic as the nights wear on
This used to be his working place

The sky over University Avenue
from my second-story window is
clean, calm, & black again in this
sudden warm night in December

Sleepily my inner voice thins
as, entering my characters' worlds,
I see all of life as unedited film
with no title, no lion, no Paramount
spangle of stars to soften what's ended,
altho everybody gets in on the credits

Far away, in the cabaret downstairs,
Asleep at the Wheel (a western country band)
breaks em up as their loud lead singer,
a little brunette with Woolworth's
in her voice, belts out, "You wanna
                take me for a ride in the
                backseat of your cawrr!"

Out on the sidewalk just below my half-
opened window three young men split
a fifth of Bali Hai & shoot the shit
& some craps 1940s-style to the music

Up here in free-lance heaven
Ive got my own floating game going on

The ante is tremendous & side bets
are OK, but youre lucky if you walk out
with the clothes on your back

December 26, 1972
Palo Alto, California
*Written three nights
before the cabaret
In Your Ear burned down*

8

The Night
Before Michael Was Born

The picture is simply chile relleno,
chicken enchilada, refried beans &
rice with lettuce salad, cold beer

by the plainest doorway, cropping out
a vanishing world we never fit into
nor of which we've ever been fans.

It's warm in here but cold outside.
Our nervous feet touch under the table.
Can the baby inside you take hot sauce?

Not Her,
She Aint No Gypsy

Fifteen years up & her tongue's still flapping
She lives in the calcium of her bones
She lives in the toughness of her liver
She lives in the memory of men she's made happy by surprise
That's her salvation for now, for the weekend

She raised a son this way but she wont get to heaven
Her heaven's got jukeboxes anyway
Lots of jukeboxes & well-peppered shot glasses, a little bush
   on the side, coin telephones
Her son's a nice kid, digs cars & girls & unh-hunh the North
   Pole, collects books & articles on it & secretly hopes to
   visit it
Just another almost American boy with a mixed-up sisterly
   mom

She was beautiful once, a wild way-out kid (as they said in
   those days) who'd try anything once, twice if it was nice
   enough
She's still beautiful in another kind of way
But she dont know this just yet
All she know is she still got ice & a lotta drink left & the
   happy-headed dude across the table say he just sold a tune
   to some rock band & they threw in a little coke to boot so
   drink up love there's plenny more where this is coming
   from baby

She gets high to connect with ecstasy & pretty soon before she
   know it everything gets to be all elemental
Even as she pulls her panties up & kisses old hairy what's-
   his-name good morning she still dont know just what it is

that's been bugging her all this time & how come her boy
turned out so straight

But that's how it go
That's just how it go
She wouldnt change now, she couldnt come down for all the
   pills in Beverly Hills, for all the booze in Veracruz

She aint sold out yet & her tongue's still flapping

The Sad Hour
of Your Peace

Elevator music from a Tokyo radio
leaks out slowly across the sand,
across greased backs, along oiled bellies
blackening in sunlight, browning, reddening

Squeezed in now, beach almost within reach,
there's no leaving right away, no casual getaway
You drove forty miles to arrive at this truce

Now there's only warm beer for refreshment
& leftover dreams to swim around & drown in
to the rise & fall of your own hot stomach
as the world breathes you in & out again

Out beyond your basic toes—the ocean,
sloshing & flashing like a liquid flame

Youre flat on your back again, goofy tunes
evaporating at your earlobes; ball-chasing
kids stomp tiptoe across your ribs
The fading glow of people you dont know
hogs up the sky & bright distances

Youre dreaming of a beach you walked alone
as a kid in a movie that was never even shot

Santa Cruz

Rediscovered Diary Entry

A glass of sweet milk
(stirred with honey)
warm by my cold Underwood

There's a woman asleep in my bed

Today I gorged myself on ice cream
& said several prayers
for energy to continue

Today I shook hands formally with
an old robed Zen master from Japan
whose head glistened youthfully
like the skin of a new golden apple
rubbed lovingly against a sleeve

Too many Aprils ago we
boarded the same bus mornings
in Berkeley with its plum blossoms
I would be on my way to work
He would simply be on his way
Today our fresh paths touched

Breathing before the pale wall of
my tiny writing room tonight,
I dissolve into all of the magazine
cutouts Ive carefully put up
to remind myself how lonely I am

Sleep must wait until daylight now
when the lady will leave for work
& I will already have done mine

Tonight in silence I sip my milk &
salute the snoring of the radiator

Today I am on my way

A Morning Poem for Michael

Where in the new fruit
lies its sweet color?
And how dare we say that
death is taking place
with such & such a being
when all the time an
ageless delight is setting in
that pleases even a
tender two-year-old?

Could it be there in
the mystery & joy we seek
& feel in connecting with
the soft flesh of others?

Visiting Day

for Conyus

This being a minimum security facility, it feels more like being on a reservation than in a touchable cage

Books are allowed, smiles, eats (you could slip a .38 inside a baked chicken or a file inside a loaf of sourdough french easily enough, but there's really not much to shoot or saw thru)

You sign up, take a seat at one of the open-air picnic tables, & yawn from hours of driving into the beautiful chilled morning

All the black inmates trudging by or hanging out of barracks windows give you the power salute as you consider yourself again strapped down in their skins

You walk, you talk, you toy around with words, you steal guarded looks down into one another

A little food, fruit juice, a lot of gossip, & the sun on the trees under blue sky surrounding us is magnified into one big silly-looking halo

"I'm not into meat all that much anymore, man, & there's a whole lotsa books I wanna talk about &—here, these're some things I wrote last month—thinking about that last letter I wrote you where I said my head was getting peaceful—what's the bloods on the block woofing about these days?"

He looks healthier than he did in the old macrobiotic city yogi wild bustling days when you'd both get zonked on sounds in the middle of the afternoon & reminisce for midnights about stuff that probably never happened

This is what's known as a conservation camp where you cut & prune trees, dig up the earth, seed the ground, weather watch, sweat a lot, do a little basketball, sun on the run, sneak peeks at crotch shots in magazines smuggled in from outside

You think of his woman, you think of his son, you think of them holed up alone in the city, waiting & waiting for him to come home

You think of all the professionals involved: pipe smokers with advanced degrees from state colleges—penologists, criminologists, sociologists who minored in deviate psychology; in clean, classy ghettos where they never take walks, their children snort coke on an allowance

Three tables away from where you sit consoling one another, a slim young man up on a burglary rap is splitting his attention between a 2-year-old daughter & a 22-year-old wife who's shown up thoughtfully in tight-fitted jeans ripped generously enough to allow him to see what she hasn't bothered wearing

Well, it isnt San Quentin, it isnt Attica, & it's no one's official prisoner of war camp, yet you cant help thinking there's a battle going on somewhere out there in the bloodstreams of men

17

You say good-bye, you shake hands good-bye, you stare good-
bye; you wave what you havent said, you grin what you
cannot say, you walk away & turn again to wave what
neither of you has to say

You gun your engine good-bye & roar off down the California
road back out into your own special prison

Weeks later you hear about the steel file some white inmate's
driven into the heart of another white inmate found by your
friend by some bushes in the rain—dead—because he was
your friend's good friend, because he was a nigger lover, a
nigger lover

The news chills the tips of your fingers & you sweat

Could it have been the father of the sweet little girl, husband
of the gal whose ass was showing?

Could it have been the marijuana dealer who read the *Bhaga-
vad Gita* & meditated nightly?

Could it have been the small-boned cat thief who spoke Spanish
with an Italian lilt like an Argentinian?

Could it have been the crinkly eyed loser who made you
laugh & laugh when he talked about his life inside & outside
the joint like a stand-up comic?

You think about the first person you ever screamed at

You think about the first thing you ever stole, or lied about,
or killed

Herrick Hospital,
Fifth Floor

for a musician friend who
finally OD'd on Blackness

Well, so youve gone & overdone it again,
overdosed yourself this time on Blackness;
locked between Blue Cross, nurse-padded walls,
the unreliable air outside & beyond
shot up with softening Berkeley sunshine

Phrasing fails you, diction cramps,
words are a loss & reflection too costly
What color were you ever but infamous blue?

If your music werent sound & its realness
didnt cleanse, I know you could never walk
much less dance out of this white room again

Green Is a Feeling,
Not a Color

In the branches of your nerves
a draft passes, as in sleep
in a storm, as the tree bends
in nights no Columbus could sail

In summer an apple shines hollow
with many suns inside it, dreaming
women swimming slowly sandy shores
in green & yellow, bikinis that smile

There's nothing new here, just
an ancient new world: a picture of
stones & flesh slipping into an ocean
into chilled kisses, caresses, as a
child would a boot or carousel spinning
with flashing pink tongues, warm teeth

Leaves of your body are flying away,
original birds, flat without mouths,
out to backyards away from the sea
across dream sand the color of burnt snow

In the branches of your nerves
leaves must only be extensions of
all our trembling treeflesh, starflesh,
the body with arms held out, a star,
five-pointed, perfect to hang space
around or light for leaf or galaxy

Love, I feel you leafless, a field
the greenness of my own invention

American
Glamour

Moss

The Rolling Stones,
a hard English group,
busted for heroin
at their Southern France estate,
fifty grams of smack a week
said the man on the news
just to keep
their little family extended

Well, so what,
whatll happen to them?
So what if the air
back of these superstars
gets waved away
from time to time
like those costly backdrops
in the old film factories?

Charles Christopher Parker,
a genius among geniuses,
was granted diplomatic immunity
the moment that he died

Eleanora Fagan Gough
(the Billie Holiday who now
powers many a Silver Cloud)
was a sufferer among sufferers
with narks up in her deathbed

Even Bela Lugosi,
our beloved Transylvanian,

sustained his habit in real life
& metaphorically on screen

Ah the Rolling Stones,
a hard English group,
heroes of an American era

Demerol

The glamour of this moment too will pass.
This bright warm wind that whispers thru me now,
thru my body, a dwelling place of spirit,
will blow itself away.

                    Like laughing gas
that dentists used in 1910 for pain,
this sweet drug even now feels out-of-date.
Is it their muzak oozing from the walls,
crisp leaves of city trees quivering with rain
outside this clinic window where I lie
that make me sad & at the same time feel
that I could swim this sinking stream of joy
forever?—no how-are-you, no good-bye.

Delicious as it seems, it doesnt last.
Having to do it over & over again
means keeping up with Joneses that dont die.

American Glamour

Is my dress appropriate?
Is my breath still fresh?
Will my underarms fail me?
What about my hair?
Should I have gotten it shaped,
is it long enough
to proclaim to one & all
my true & lasting blackness?

It's the 7 A.M. flight.
Even the plane seems to yawn
as they test its engines
one by one in the historic fog of
San Francisco International.

The stewardesses in their
miniskirted uniforms,
designed by some promotional committee
to make them look pretty & sexy,
look silly, look shot, look
O so American cheesecake!

There arent enough minutes
between now & landing to
savor these ridiculous niceties:
coffee in flight, token sweet roll,
documentary voice of the pilot
droning the time, temperatures,
            altitudes, cruising speeds. . . .

Dozing amid commuters who'd fall
into deep sleep if they only knew

they were up here with a poet
trying to play his nuttiness down,
I'm on my way to interview
the great Ray Charles on assignment.

Pacific Southwest Airlines into L.A. today
—tomorrow? Who knows? Trans World!

Roland Navarro (1939–1961)

I leave you on that downtown street of
how many Detroit winters ago, standing
in front of the March of Dimes display
in a window, wincing aloud to me of suffering
people all over the world where a boy
cut out of cardboard on crutches implores,
"Please won't you help? Please won't you give?"

You were home from West Point, the holidays,
still owing me a big bottle of vodka from
some high-school bet that's as dark & forgotten
as any old joke from the shadowy past.

You wanted to be a big general down in
South America, Argentina, where your skilled dad
took refuge after twenty years of visiting you
weekends at his parents' home, your grand-
parents' house on Clairmount not far from
12th Street where we each caught buses, sometimes
together, & lived straight out of our heads
littered with print, pictures, & old pianos—
you Chicano, me black, both of us niggers.

We loved the same girls more than once &
you wrote in a letter how I should think twice
about becoming a poet or artist of any kind
because the mad world had no more need of
that kind of craziness: *"They grind you down
and fuck you around, then toss you a crumb or
a well-gnawed bone, then shit on you again."*

You told me, *"Be a soldier, be an ass kicker,*
& get in on the take by starting at the top."

How many times we played your Napoleon game
with paper ships & troops in war-torn Novembers!
Cursing like a sailor, upsetting my mother,
you wrote enough of an epic novel to impress
the hell out of me along with your drawings
& that piano piece of yours called *Funeral Bells.*
I still have the portrait you did of me when
I was studying trumpet—*Young Horn with a Boy.*

So your father remarried, a woman more our age,
leaving you with snapshots of your mother,
a legend who died before you'd learned to love.
I leave you watery-eyed in front of that paper
publicity cripple, you who wanted to rule men
tall in your shiny black Argentine boots,
frightened by a tenderness your heart couldnt rule.
Here the world ends, here the sun's hidden
forever from a scene you abandoned slyly
to return to your bright new Connecticut love
whose photo you flashed reminded me of
your lost mamá & a princess named Juanita
(uncrowned object of our junior-high search)
but this sure-enough Her Highness was rich
& fair.
               Come that summer you'd finally marry
the goddess you always accused me of seeking.

You did it, you did it, you outfoxed fate!
You survived the honor system & graduated clean.
I looked forward to studying you in histories
to come but the world & impatience got in the way.
All that Pérez Prado we'd been thru together,

all that Mingus, Debussy, *Swan Lake* & the Penguins,
Rimbaud, Charlie Parker, Tolstoi, Cézanne, Joe Loco
wasnt enough to head off an ending I'd rather
imagine than know as I did Vivian or Nina,
as I know the moon of honey Mexico where you died
in an auto crash that killed you outright &
left your bride crippled like that poster child.

I think of you always, I even hum your song
here where what's right must collide with what's wrong.

1961–1973

Ho

She coulda been somethin
like the Supremes or somebody
Her folks give her everything she need
I use to know her family pretty good
They dont have that much but they
   aint on relief
She call herself in love

Her money it go for that stuff, I guess,
   & for strong mouthwash, I know
I see her buyin Baby Ruths & Twinkies too
   down at the liquor store

Every night she start her day
right under my window when the lights
   come on
She aint bad-lookin neither, just little

She just a skinny little sister
bout big as my fist
but even she done slipped & found out
heaven aint the only H in the dictionary

Making Love After Hours

Back up in the room they snap on
all-nite movies but leave the sound
turned down, turned off.
                              You see,
neon & smoke last just so long & soon
there're no more joints to haunt
or get lost in, no more ghosts to give up
except the flicker & ripple of TV light
against their shot bodies quivering with shadow.

With an urgency of children permitted to
stay up way past bedtime, they share,
they linger, they nurse the last drink.
They whisper & they whisper, sighing to collapse.

She peels off her turtleneck,
undoes her jeans, kicks her sandals
straight toward the window as the moon comes up
shining thru clouds in a rainy 1930s
tight-suit movie, too mellow a moon,
like some yawning display in a budget-store window.

For week & weeks he's dragged around feeling
sorry for himself but now unalone, naked
next to her, he just cant remember how much
        or how come.

Two stories down, drunks stumble the streets
in search of some phone booths to pee in.

Realism

Socialist Realism & Capitalist Realism
are the same thing

I am thinking this way &
walking down Shattuck with my wife
when I catch the sign in
Woolworth's window

Lifelike
PLASTIC
FLOWERS
with
built-in-bloom
washable
nonallergic
prices
as marked
Satisfaction Guaranteed
or
money refunded

So knowing a good poem
when I see one I copy it down
on the back of the brown envelope
from the Telephone Company that says—
EXTENSION PHONES take the run
out of RUNNING A HOME!

Head of a Woman

That gypsy strain is
daubed into her eyes

the hair brushed on
so blackly with care

brown face brown neck
round jaw wide face

smooth stylized ear
with airy ring of cloud

at its lobe for decor.
Her mouth is that full

human-lipped love mouth
ripe & sensuous, as they say

in poems, but which painters
show. The green shawl

she's been wearing slips
down to delight us with

a bundle of shoulder also
brown, brown the color

brown the evening air
framed ever so softly

in breathable surroundings
of imaginary light.

Geography of the Near Past

Manhattan March, The 1970s

A black teenager strapped to
the baby boy on her back
straight out the South or some
unnoticed Connecticut slum
crowded with media promise
steps up to ask me one midnight
if I know a hotel nearby in
the neighborhood where they can
put up for the night reasonable

How bout the Chelsea?
Tried it but they want too much!

Too much is involved
Too much anger
Too much softness

Her lovely hard eyes
look way down into me

I know the no-man's-land
she's running away from by now

Stop some driver &
ask the taxi, I say,
which she does cautiously
over my skyscraped shoulder

The world is you
The world is me

The world is you with
me strapped to its back

37

Fun City Samba

for Ann McIntosh

Even being able to get a glimpse of moon
in a sky tacked up over West 22nd Street
that I didnt know existed in New York
is motive enough for celebration

What do I do next, is it proper to smile?
Is it bad city form to whistle & jangle
gently as you walk (like Satchel Paige says)
to keep the juices flowing, to avoid running
at all times?

        Ive almost never looked back
on myself in this city designed so much
for the moment that even the pain of peeking
out the window at 2 A.M. to check out a
modishly pantsuited, fortyish woman swearing
& crying, bumping into parked cars,
screaming up at the window of a lover
she almost got together with in the bar
around the corner is only instant Off-B'way

East Boston

for Denise Levertov

Up in this warm, solid house of yours
while you make breakfast I stand sighing
at the window, breaths away from
this working-class block where trash cans
lined up in front of old buildings
look natural with sun shining down on them

If my heart seems to leap from my shirt
away away away from this instant it's
because the short drive in from Logan Airport
thru last night's minute of neighborhood
streetlight with children playing in it
is whisking me back thru my decades again

Way past dark we chased one another
We had our own style of stickball too
when the England you smiled in wasnt so new

If my voice is quivering it's also because
the sky up over your Boston Inner Harbor
is too splendid to look at this morning—
cool waters below, those barges so sober!

Ive lived for so long now on another coast

Providence, Rhode Island

It's spring again
the early part when
the wettest wind
gives you a licking
youll never forget

You stand quivering
down by the Biltmore
whistling for taxis
as maxiskirted women
flee the scene
youve just stepped into

The grayness of this
white water city feels
good to blood that wants
to explode on century's notice
shattering calendar meat
& appointments well kept

Colonial afternoons
had to be colder than
the hearts of witches
laid to rest beneath
these charming city paved hills

Rushing for cover
you now understand the
cooled-out literalness
of these old wooden homes

A skinny black man
(a brother you guess)
who commutes between
this stop & Harlem U.S.A.
tells you he's never been to
Brown or the School of Design
but he know for a fact that
it's Mafia keep this town relaxed

"They got the highest houses
up in them hills but after them
come all your professors & professionals, people with a
high-class license to steal"

You want to come back in
summer when the change takes
place but this brilliant chill
has tightened your head

New England is a poker game too

New Orleans Intermission

*"A lighted window holds me like
high voltage. I see . . ."*
WALTER BENTON,
This Is My Beloved

1

I see it zooming down
over the bayou late April
morning of the brightest green
from the window of a jet named Nancy

Settling back childishly
in the sky all alone,
my secret hand waves light aside
to get a better look at
all the music coiling up
inside me again as I watch
this still virgin landscape

Is that the famous Mississippi
down there, are those the streets
Jelly Roll did his marching,
strutting, & poolsharking in?
Was I really just born
a gulf away from here or
carved like Pinocchio
from some thick dark tree below?

2

The only way to love a city's
to live in it till you know
every door every store every

parkingmeter deadlawn alleycat
district smell pussy hotel
gumwrapper & wino by heart

Airborne all night my sleepy heart
leaps like windblown raindrops

I'm a very old baby reentering
an unchanged world with a yawn

3

Yes Ive lived here before
just as I know & can feel in my tongue
that Ive tramped this earth as
storyteller & unaccountable thief
too many times before,
a displaced lover of spirit & flesh

Riding the St. Charles trolley nights
an old American, classically black,
spots me as a tourist & softly explains
how he dont have to take snapshots
no more since he can more or less
picture in his mind what's keepable

When I take this 15¢ ride, the cool
off-hour breeze tightening my skin,
I can tune in to people telling their
stories real slow in the form of asides
& catch myself doing a lot of smiling
to hold back tears

                    Old-timer tells me
why the fare on this line's so cheap:

"It's so the colored maids & cooks &
gardeners can git to they jobs & back
without it bein a strain on they pocket"

     4

On Bourbon Street (North Beach or
Times Square) a fan-tailed redhead in
G-string & nothing else waves me
into a topless/bottomless joint with a
dog-faced barker posted at the door
who yips & howls: "C'mon in yall & see
southron gals takin off they draws
for just the price of a drink!"

                         It isnt
enough to laugh & rush in like a
prospective drunk that's in heat

The point is that love & love alone
holds up my feet as they step from
Bourbon to Rampart Street, dreaming of
Congo Square, Creole intrigue, Fats
Domino & Dr John while a black panhandler
(cross between Satchmo & Papa John Creach)
hits on me for 50¢ in front of Al Hirt's

     5

Steaming hot down in front of us now:
ham biscuit eggs grits Cajun coffee
& a solid glass of buttermilk for me
for fun—

          It's Mama's in the morning
where American poet Miller Williams

44

leans past his dark wife, Becky, to say:
"You probly the only Californian that
really knows about this place, man"

I know I'll slip back by for gumbo,
for lunch known down here as dinner,
or for a supper of 90¢ crawfish bisque

But right now it's the light quivering
in from the street down onto our plates
that makes us quit talking poetry

"I'd give up writing," Miller sighs,
"if I could sing as good as Ray Charles"

Tomorrow theyll drive back to the Ozarks
Tomorrow I'll fly back to California
where there're no nickel phone calls,
pick up the show from where I left off
& read Marie Laveau the Voodoo Queen

City Home/Detroit

Old emotions like powdery tenements
undulate in the July heat.
It would take an ocean of sentiment
to cool your memories of this street
that first contained your notions of how
the world operates, how it is what it is.

How your body sweats & pours now
as it prepares to deal with the quiz
that's been haunting you all these years
of walking the earth, stepping thru time,
refining your eyesight, opening your ears
for a liberating music, scales you can climb.

What if you never had run from this race
(Cleveland to Detroit to Chicago, New York)?
What if you'd settled & stayed in your place
among friends who'd never arrive at that fork
in the road of their flat midwestern lives
where Atlantic & Pacific equals A & P,
where rock salt's for winter, & when summer arrives
wish for showers to ease the humidity?

In your California sandals & flowery shirt,
hair a juicy network of coils & strands,
hoping today you wont get robbed or hurt,
you know what forced you to seek other lands.

Dude in Denver

This skinny little dude
up next to a mountain
(the Rockies, eastern slope)
with his wimp mouth look,
cap not even fitting
his pointed head right

His lips hang out from his
mouth & kinda to one side
so when he talk they flap
just enough so you can spot him
from grand distances

He takes a sip of 7Up
from a can swiped from a truck,
adjusts the floppy collar of
his leather coat & Big Apple cap,
blinks behind winter shades
as a cold-blooded Lincoln snores by

Skied over, he undergoes a change
of nerve, looking over both shoulders
to make sure no one's watching
before approaching the parked bike
left unlocked by some college-looking
white girl who could show up any
minute to blow the whistle for good
on this good thing he thinks he's got

Oppression? Repression? Suppression?
Depression? The pressure he's under,

were it ever let out, might heat up
this windblown November afternoon

Can he really be as sad as he looks
now, hunched over in need of a ten-speed
bicycle, cheerless, thin, a thief so
leery of anything passing in the light
within reach of his wet, greedy eyes?—

A Colorado colored boy, Afro, American,
a downright American little dude

Any Inner City Blues

It would be so easy,
afternoons particularly,
to go take that leap
off the Golden Gate
or run full speed head-on
into the legendary path
of anyone's unpaid-for auto
or shoot up a tablespoon of smack
& lie down in the middle of
the James Lick Memorial Freeway

Or to be modern,
contemporary at least—
give your heart to know
folly & false daring:
race thru the ruins of what was
hip once, pollinating flowerchildren
          at large;
small visible recompense for
a hurt that burns to be eradicated,
not multiplied, like
the head-splitting cancer
that surrounds you

Mexico City Lover

for Matt Kahn

Going back to D.F.
soon as he can
take a pesero
down the Reforma
straight to her
dollar hotel,
bottle of Bacardi
under one arm
& his heart under
the other beating
like the wings
of a fearful chicken
in the arms
of its raiser
on a third-class bus
to the city

While the kids're
grabbing at balloons
in Chapultepec Park
& the chicks're
snapping Chiclets
in rosy-roofed mouths
he'll slip his free arm
around her waist &
jaywalk her to heaven
under the hefty
smog-prevention trees
limb around trunk
trucks whizzing past
while vaudeville horns
jam traffic music

They can more than
work it on out,
the town'll be theirs
the hours their pink zone
shadows & all
the pulse-stopping dawn
an unfillable trophy
of light for some
a toucher of others
as they kiss in the bowels
of a city neither
of them has chosen for
home on this clay ball
in this stone & steel
Tenochtitlán love nest

California Peninsula:
El Camino Real

In 15 minutes
the whole scene'll change
as bloated housewives
hems of their skirts greased
with love mouths wide open
come running out of shops
dragging their young
moon in their eyes
the fear upon them

Any minute now
the gas-blue sky over El Camino Real
is going to droop for good
shut with a squish &
close them all in like
a giant irritated eye

Theyll scramble for cars
the nearest road out
clutching their steering wheels
like stalwart monkeys

It couldve happened yesterday
It couldve happened while they
were sighing in Macy's Walgreen's 31 Flavors
Copenhagen Movies or visiting the Colonel
like that earthquake night
that shattered L.A.

Whatll they will their children then?
Whatll they leave for them to detest?

What tree, what lip print, what Jack in
what Box, what ugly hot order to go?

Already I can smell the darkness
creeping in like the familiar shadow
of some beloved fake monster
in a science fiction flick

In 15 minutes
48 hours days weeks months
years from now all of thisll be
a drowsy memory barely tellable
in a land whose novelty was speech

Geography of the Near Past

The trick
without anyone's
catching on to it
is to swim against
world current
knowing it to be as much a dream
as it is drama on the highest stage
but without losing touch
with spirit or with light

Realer even
is to move as if
nothing has ever happened
which is likewise
as true as foam or fog

Each universe is only
an ever-shifting sea
in the surfacing eyes of former fish

Some
Recent
Fiction

"How do we separate fiction from reality?
Medical students recited Galen
to the effect that some particular bone
belonged to the breast at the very moment
it was being extracted from the foot."

EVAN S. CONNELL,
Points for a Compass Rose

Some Recent Fiction

1

He ran his hands thru her hair
slowly
as tho he were relishing the feel
of expensive Italian corduroy.
The light of Venus did a little dance
way over in the eastern sky.
"Spring again,"
she murmured,
moving herself thru water
soft brown breasts bobbing gingerly
sending electric symbols thru him,
for the extent of his naïveté
was a pubic thing
known publicly by his mother.
Zara is running thru fields of poppies,
she scoops five fingers of cool earth
& rubs it into her cheeks
in fierce denial of her albescence,
funky cloud passing over the moon itself.
"Get it on,
you little s'pose-to-be white girl!"
shouts Superspook in a fit of pique.
He knew her other lover,
the very pig who represented
all white savagery to him,
cloaked society
that by dint of respectability could . . .
The Pig can always move in brother
with his heavy weapons

& blow us away
—his ultimate fear revisiting him,
cool young girl trembling
under his hard erotic touch.
"Hell I'll up & make me an anthem of my own!"
the black voice was heard to declare
cutting thru the narcotic haze of memory
that shimmered over the room to the very
stained-glass windows
built on bitter black sweat.
A little thing drifted back from childhood,
he knew at last the meaning of meaning,
thoughts of wilderness
& the touch of what was
& what was not sexual
purely
a little dream victory galloping thru him.
"I love you, Hitler."
She remembered that phrase
spoken in earnest
& established
by white-haired literati
whom she had once esteemed
in her windblown university days
at Bootlick State.

The two men & the girl
at sunrise
writhed quietly
in rock agony
as the radio clock
buzzed & bounced with all the beats.

All skies fizzled.

2

It is the time of the prosaic showdown.
Noon & Dickens brighten her bones.
She knew the time was coming
when she would be required to brandish a gun
& wave it in the face of even best friends,
of poor Agnes the pathetic acid
head
in whose loins
the Afro-Anglo-Indian milieu
revolved like an IBM typewriter ball
splattering piecemeal
her spiralworm tape-code genetics
more complex than thunderbird circuitry
made naked
by degrees.
"If I had my way
I would lick the very white from your eyes
I would
& jet you away up & out of this melting pot
become pressure cooker,"
he pronounced
reminding her of Thad
when they were first wed
in office-worker Cleveland
the 35¢ wedding soup
& his acting their only hope
her city welfare childhood
Pa packing them all up to them opportunity
cities the smoke choking
even the sodas had soot on the surface
& overpsychoanalyzed Frederick
poor chump seeking to seduce
her irate Trinidadian stepmother

before the blue of her world
turned ashen rose
wind cutting thru
her mind
like lust
the baby so far away
the FM loneliness
Scotches & marijuanas Rod would bring.
Thad would wound her if he found out
cold blade of life cutting
her down & opening up her vegetable heart,
the uneaten orders
unheard ballads
undusted shelves
the tinned fruits & soups on shelves,
the jolly green giantess
trembling in the world air
that closes in
like a trap,
like a suburb
Tuesdays.

3

I shot my sweet tongue down into her craw
& pulled the knife from its heart of veins
everything happening & running
together like blood.
Zara, if you love me
kiss this manuscript
take me back thru guillotine days
the women hanging all off me
the gambles I took
to come out straight
a bright-haired

bright-eyed advocate
of everything interesting
interesting & healthy
the healthy films that are going to be made
the big tits
box office
the way they forced me into Confederate uniforms
the perils of Atlantic
guns my ma left me in her will
to shoot down Billy
time time you thrilled me in Rome
& the ravishing beans they kept pushing on me
in New Orleans.
Kiss me with your Quasimodo lips
hug me Raskolnikov
press me to your bosom Che.
If you will soothe me
just a shade more
I will tell you why our president
deserves the medal more than Zeus,
I will tell you
why I love my own consciousness
more than anything
& we can set the puke-
colored flag of
all inferior countries
out to dry
on windowsills of the word
the world enemy
& map some neocolonialist pimp
gentle reader
creep who buys my hustle.
Kiss this revolutionary on the lips,
everybody tingling,
you must esteem me perfectly

in the passes Ive made toward Virtue
& if I flounder ever
it is because everyman
adores himself
in my new city skin.

Teaching

There's no such thing as a student,
only abiding faces unwilling
to change except with time,
the oldest force that still fools us

So you teach a feeling,
a notion learned the hard way,
a fact, some figures,
a tract, some rigors of childhood

The face out there
interacting with yours
knows how to grin & play with its pen
but misses the point so charmingly

A thousand moves later
that same shiny face
moving thru the world with
its eyes glazed or fully closed
reconnects with one of its own childhoods

Loosely we call this learning

The New Mystic

The waters I'm going to go walking beside,
vibrations Ive been taking into my system,
the cool nourishing breeze,
the living browns & greeneries
waving in the wind around me,
the real men & women
with whom I keep in touch,
our souls poking out
like bone
thru serious wounds,
the basic, familiar smell of life
raw or uncooked
breathed in thru nostrils
or exhaled thru tenderer membranes
—proof flowing back to me
that there's only one Dreamer:
the playful faddist & mystery lover
who sees me thru these boogies & tangos
whose steps & movements
seem to get made up
somehow as I go along

Aunt

She talks too loud, her face
a blur of wrinkles & sunshine
where her hard hair shivers
from laughter like a pine tree
stiff with oil & hotcombing

O & her anger realer than gasoline
slung into fire or lighted mohair
She's a clothes lover from way back
but her body's too big to be chic
or on cue so she wear what she want
People just gotta stand back &
take it like they do Easter Sunday when
the rainbow she travels is dry-cleaned

She laughs more than ever in spring
stomping the downtowns, Saturday past
work, looking into JC Penney's checking
out Sears & bragging about how when she
feel like it she gon lose weight &
give up smokin one of these sorry days

Her eyes are diamonds of pure dark space
& the air flying out of them as you look
close is only the essence of living
to tell, a full-length woman, an aunt
brown & red with stalking the years

Cherokees

Brave Indian warrior
I'm glad I sawr ya

Now, that's the way I like to start singing "Cherokee," which is a fine song I think and one day I shall learn all the correct words.

Ray Noble, an Englishman, wrote "Cherokee" long before I dropped into the century. I cant help wondering what kind of waves his mind or heart might have been radiating at the time.

Historical Note: "In 1762 three Cherokee chiefs appeared in London as picturesque ambassadors. Indian reprisals for acts of lawless frontiersmen had marred English-Cherokee relations; but a year after the Indians' visit to England, whites and reds signed a treaty of friendship," it says in *The American Heritage Book of Indians*.

Ah, the unlikeliness of world lore. It was Charlie Parker of course who first pulled me into the song itself on his faithful old Savoy recording of it when I was a dreamy adolescent addicted to the various musicks. Nights I'd sit in my window and behold that tune growing brighter and brighter in the light of all that light Mr. Parker kept bringing to it. He called it "Ko-Ko," and all the famous Jazz writers like to re-jot what Mr. Parker told them was in his mind and heart around the time he was getting his ideas about "Cherokee" together, starting around December 1939 (I'd been back on earth six months): Yardbird's in the back room of that Harlem Chili House "jamming" with Biddy Fleet, the guitar player, so Bird, quite naturally, like each of us, has a very special message he has been getting ready to drop on the public for quite some time. "I could hear it sometimes but I couldnt play it!"

Then he got on into "Cherokee."

History.

It's all history. We're all history.

The trees and stones are history.

Moon is history.

It all keeps meeting at the moment, yet we are fond of believing ourselves to be the center of all creation.

To further simplify matters, Cherokee is also the name of one of God's creations I first heard about after school when all the kids would stand around the doors and high wire fence to smoke cigarettes and make fun of everything.

This girl I knew would say, "Well, what I like about Cherokee is he got a whole lot of soul, know what I mean? Cherokee look you dead in your eye when he talk and he pretty sincere too about what he gon do—if he go for you. Like, the time he told Mr. Crookshank right out loud in class, told him right to his face he was prejudiced and he was gon personally whip his butt first chance he got, so Mr. Crookshank get all uptight and jiggedy and take Cherokee up to the principal and tell him what Cherokee say, tell him this boy threatened me in class, so Mr. Brown ask Cherokee did he really say that, so Cherokee say, 'That's correct, you heard right, I'mo go up side this gentleman's head if he dont start havin some respect for all us students irregardless of race, color, or creed.' "

"Yeah and what about that time he stole the police car over on Linwood while the cops was sittin up in Stafford's eatin dinner and there was Cherokee ridin up and down the block playin the siren and when the cops come out to see who it was they dont find out nothin cause by that time Cherokee done eased the short on round the corner and parked it and gone on bout his business."

"Unnh-hunh, I knew about that but what about the time over at the Greystone Ballroom when Cool Breeze and Captain Midnight and them was drinkin all that bad wine talkin bout how they was gon turn the place out in a few minutes

soon as they drink some more wine and Cool Breeze talkin
bout he was so bad and got two brothers run with the Shakers*
and then after they finish drinkin wine they started messin
with Cherokee's broad, man, Rennie, and you know Cherokee
he pretty peaceful till people get to messin over him and he
know Cool Breeze and them is drunk so he tell em they better
be cool, so then they wouldnt stop so Cherokee snatch they
little bottle of wine away from em and him and his boys turns
out the Greystone in fifteen-twenty minutes, and Cool Breeze
and Captain Midnight and them was supposed to be so bad."

His girl friend Rennie (Renée) lived not too far from
me: a lean, comely, redheaded gal whose mama'd get drunk
and beat her up all the time or lock her out of the house when
she'd come in too late. Rennie luhhhved Cherokee and was
wise to the fact that any of the ordinary girls would gratefully
walk from Windsor, Ontario, all the way to Detroit, Michigan,
to say "Hi" to him any day. Rennie herself was no ordinary
young lady. She always figured that if push came to shove she
could always strut those freckles on out to Hollywood and sign
on as a starlet. "My old lady dont dig me because she knows
I'm cute, but that's all right—long as I got Cherokee."

Cherokee's thing seemed to be to show up for classes
when there was absolutely nothing else doing. You'd see him
and then he'd be gone. First time I saw him, someone else was
pointing him out to me. "Well, there he go, man."

"There go who?"

"There go Cherokee."

"So that's Cherokee?"

"That is *the* Cherokee. You mean to tell me you didnt
know who Cherokee was?"

"Look, I feel like I was born knowin Cherokee but I
only just now switched over to this school a little while ago."

"Well, *I'll* excuse you but if I was you I wouldnt go

* A major gang in the history of Detroit, from the 1950s.

round tellin too many people I didnt know who Cherokee was."

"O I knew who he was all right, I just wasnt sure which one he was."

"Cherokee been tryna get outta this junior high school a whole lot longer'n it's taken you to get in."

"What's the matter with him?"

"He aint got good sense."

"How come?"

"How come you ask me somethin like that? Man, I dont know—he just aint got good sense. He a Indian, maybe Indians aint suppose to have good sense. Of course he part Spook too. I dont know, but I tell you one thing: dont nobody be messin with him."

So much for hearsay. I met up with him in an art class one semester and he was very quiet and dutiful, did his little drawings, always had a good word for everyone, took his work very seriously. Then he went and got into another one of those bizarre situations and was thrown out of school again. Fortunately, I ran up on him again at La Fiesta, a short-lived non-Mexican rib parlor on 12th Street. He bought me Pepsi-Cola and he said, "Man, I like you. Guess you see me all the time gettin into trouble with my mouth and fightin and carryin on but I know what I wanna do. I wanna do the same thing everybody else wanna do, you know? Wanna just be cool, you know? Just draw and sing and stuff and get along with everybody and be cool. That aint askin too much is it? But the people wont leave me alone, look like all they wanna do's keep messin with me. But you just wait and see, just keep watchin, man, I'mo make it. I shall be cool and do my thing dont care how long it take. I'm in a little trouble right now but that wont stop me."

A few months later Cherokee got busted—I forget for what, burglary or something—and was sent away to be reformed. I have never seen him again, but every time I hear the song or get to whistling it, I often flicker back thru dreams to that April afternoon to the exact place where he removed his shades and looked me dead in the eye to say, "I'm in a little trouble right now but that wont stop me."

I was also reminded of him when a middle-aged Cherokee Indian on the number 43 bus to Oakland last Christmas told the dark little girl plopped by me, says, "Ha ha, you a nigger, you dont come from here, your people dont come from here, you not like me, you from Africa."

So she huffs herself up gently and says: "And just where do you think you come from?"

He was drunk.
We are all drunk
with self-hatred
one time or another,
how else can we go on
hating one another?

Poetry

It is possible to rest here.
It is possible to arrive home
headed this way
thru the wind & rain of this night
alone
to a place where starlight
isnt the point.
It is true that we are orphans
under the skin
where fluids combine
& organisms function intelligently,
where vision or sound
in image or vibration
need only be true
to spark the way there.
There is here & always was.
You sniff & clear your throat
in this unintentional night
borrowed from eternity
or let yourself be saddened by nothing.
I sit in a white kitchen
next to the young walls,
yellow paper spread on yellow tablecloth,
& scratch helplessly,
wanting to take new leave
of the present
which was a gift,
longing to have known everything
& to have been everywhere
before the world dissolves
a tangle of journeys

& messages
unrecorded
undeciphered
wrinkled down into me.

Boogie with
O.O. Gabugah

Note

O.O. Gabugah writes that he "was born in a taxicab right smack on 125th and Lenox in Harlem on Lincoln's Birthday, 1945. Franklin Delano Watson was the name my poor brainwashed parents gave me but I had that racist tag legally altered once I got old enough to see what was going down. The O.O., by the way, stands for Our Own, i.e., we need to do *our own* thing, can you dig it?"

In addition to being one of our strongest young Black revolutionary voices, Brother Gabugah is the author of half a dozen volumes, all of which have appeared since last year. *Slaughter the Pig & Git Yo'self Some Chit'lins* is the title of his most popular work which is presently in its sixth big printing. Other volumes include: *Niggers with Knives, Black on Back, Love Is a White Man's Snot-Rag* and *Takin Names and Kickin Asses.* His plays—*Transistor Willie & Latrine Lil* and *Go All the Way Down & Come Up Shakin* (a revolutionary Black musical)—received last month's Drama Authority Award.

The brother is presently the recipient of both a Federal Arts Agency grant as well as a Vanderbilt Fellowship to conduct research on Richard Wright. Currently vacationing in Australia, he is preparing a collection of critical essays tentatively titled *Woodpile Findings: Cultural Investigations into What's Goin On.*

His last critical work, *Nothin Niggers Do Will Ever Please Me,* is also a favorite.

"O.O. Gabugah draws strong folk poetry from the voice of a strident but vital revolutionary who attacks the Uncle Tom," states *The Nation* in its March 19, 1973, issue.

A militant advocate of the oral tradition, he chooses to dictate his poems through me rather than write them down himself.

The Old O.O. Blues

Like right now it's the summertime
   and I'm so all alone
I gots to blow some fonky rhyme
   on my mental saxophone

Brother Trane done did his thang
   and so have Wes Montgomery,
both heavyweights in the music rang,
   now I'mo play my summary

It's lotsa yall that thank yall white
   (ought I say European?)
who thank Mozart and Bach's all right,
   denyin your Black bein

Well, honkyphiles, yall's day done come,
   I mean we gon clean house
and rid the earth of Oreo scum
   that put down Fats for Faust

This here's one for-real revolution
   where aint nobody playin
We intends to stop this cultural pollution
   Can yall git to what I'm sayin?

Sittin up there in your Dior gown
   and Pierre Cardin suit
downtown where all them devil clowns
   hang out and they aint poot!

We take the white man's bread and grants
   but do our own thang with it

76

while yall bees itchin to git in they pants
and taint the true Black spirit

I'm blowin for Bird and Dinah and Billie,
for Satch, Sam Cooke, and Otis,
for Clifford, Eric, and Trane outta Philly
who split on moment's notice

Chump, you aint gon never change,
your narrow ass is sankin
Like Watergate, your shit is strange
You drownin while we thankin

My simple song might not have class
but you cant listen with impunity
We out to smash your bourgeois ass
and by *we* I mean The Community!

Black Queen
for More Than a Day

I thirst for
    the Kool-Aid
  of your fabulous
fine fruit-flavored throat

Lick that ebony tongue
    out at me
  and let that licorice
  divine heavenly lickrish
    slide down my system

Chocolate mama, *mmm mmm*

Beauty is to boodie as
  class struggle is
    to ass struggle
  so let's git it on
for the night is long

When you place your hot dark arm
    cross my chest
    I'm like
some fierce tribal warrior
    ready to git
  down to natural bizness

With my head held high
    I walk through the sky
      with its cornrow of stars
and you scroonched all

                up next to me
                        sweet as you are

I'm the original poet
        (and I damn well know it)
        when you suckle me,
                you stallion you

Black woman
        my African Queen
                for more than a day
        kiss me with your
                Congo
                lips

What You Seize
Is What You Git

You must thank
  yo dookey don't stank
    while you be's gittin high
     up in the sky
  of yo hand-
          ker-
             chief
                head
    home, nigga,
  you sorryass muthafucka,
swillin slop at the white beast's
      trough
  (like black aint down enough),
   payin taxes insteada
     grindin axes,
  slurpin up all that Boone's Farm
    Strawberry Hill
    (oughtta be called hell)
     wine,
   you wind-up, computerized
    Sambo

   You look like somethin
    outta Tarzan
  just cant wait to sniff Jane's titty,
    thinkin you pretty,
  but you aint nothin, nigga,
  you and yo old lady workin
    4 jobs 7 days a week
     & wont even speak
     up for yo rights

day or night
just so yo pickaninny chile
can grow up and run the mile
in the racist Olympics,
oil for yall to slide for a ride
on into the middle class

Well, all yall can kiss my revolutionary ass!

We tireda niggas buyin Cholly's wine and cars
and neckties and bell-bottoms and yes books
and bein bused to his plastic schools
to learn how to be some white kinda fool

We talkin bout hackin the bleached-out devil
to pieces
& shippin Chunks-O-Hunky out to Venus
for the interplanetary brothers
up there to chaw on, muthas,
you sassyass beautiful black muthas
tryin to fare well on welfare

Quit playin with yo'self, nigga, & come!
Come on back into the warm black fold
that aint got nothin to do with gold

Come on back where we at and *live*, i.e.,
lib-er-rated, de-*live*-ered
from tyranny!

Come on back where we rezides
greaze on some greens
and check some sides—

Shoot ol Pharoah
(and we dont mean Brother Sanders)

in the butt with yo poisoned Kikuyu arrow
unless you tryna be the knee-grow Ann Landers . . .

It still aint too late
to keep the fate, Gate!

Write on, Bruh,
with yo funky baaaaaad-ass
Afro-headed
self!

Paris/ Dar-es-Salaam
1972

A Poem for Players

Yes, theyll let you play,
let you play third base or fender bass,
let you play Harrah's Club or Shea Stadium

Theyll let you play
in a play anyway: Shakespeare,
Ionesco, Bullins, Baraka, or Genet,
only dont get down *too* much
& dont go gettin too uppity

Theyll let you play,
oh yes, on the radio, stereo,
even on the video, Ojays,
O.J. Simpson, only please dont stray
too far from your ghetto rodeo

Theyll let you be Satchmo,
theyll let you be Diz,
theyll let you be Romeo,
   or star in *The Wiz*
but you gots to remember that
   that's all there is

Oh, you can be a lawyer or a medico,
a well-briefcased executive with Texaco;
you can even get yourself hired, man,
to go teach *Ulysses* in Dublin, Ireland

Theyll let you play
so long as you dont play around,
so long as you play it hot or cool,

so long as you dont play down the blues
theyll let you play in *Playboy*, *Playgirl*,
    or the *Amsterdam News*

Finally theyll let you play
politics if you dont get in the way
the way some of us did and had to be
iced by conspiracy, international mystery

Theyll let you play anybody but you,
that's pretty much what they will do